LEWIS AND CLARK

MAP THE AMERICAN WEST

By Nel Yomtov

Illustration By Joel Vollmer

Color By Gerardo Sandoval

Black Sheep

BELLWETHER MEDIA · MINNEAPOLIS, MN

STRAY FROM REGULAR READS
WITH BLACK SHEEP BOOKS.
FEEL A RUSH WITH EVERY READ!

Library of Congress Cataloging-in-Publication Data

Yomtov, Nelson.
  Lewis and Clark Map the American West / by Nel Yomtov.
      pages cm. -- (Black Sheep: Extraordinary Explorers)
  Summary: "Exciting illustrations follow the events of the Lewis and Clark expedition. The combination of brightly colored panels and leveled text is intended for students in grades 3 through 7"-- Provided by publisher.
  Audience: Ages 7 to 12
  In graphic novel form.
  Includes bibliographical references and index.
  ISBN 978-1-62617-293-7 (hardcover: alk. paper)
  1. Lewis and Clark Expedition (1804-1806)--Juvenile literature. I. Title.
  F592.Y66 2016
  917.804'2--dc23
                              2015002650

This edition first published in 2016 by Bellwether Media, Inc.

Printed in the United States of America, North Mankato, MN.

TABLE OF CONTENTS

Orange text identifies *historical quotes.*

THE JOURNEY BEGINS

May 21, 1804:
Meriwether Lewis and William Clark set out from St. Charles, Missouri. They have been chosen to lead an **expedition** to explore the Louisiana Territory.

President Thomas Jefferson bought the Louisiana Territory from France the year before. Now he wants to learn more about the new land.

MERIWETHER LEWIS

WILLIAM CLARK

Lewis was a captain in the U.S. Army. Then he became President Jefferson's secretary. Clark had been Lewis's commanding officer in the Army.

That would give a direct route to the Pacific Ocean!

We will follow the Missouri River to its source. Hopefully it links with the Columbia River in the northwest.

Lewis and Clark have a team of more than 30 men for the expedition. The group calls itself the **Corps** of Discovery. They have spent many months preparing for the journey.

The **keelboat** and two **pirogues** are packed with food, cooking tools, and weapons. They also bring medical supplies and scientific instruments.

This could be a big boost for the fur trade.

Hopefully we can build friendships with the people we meet.

Mouth of the Columbia River

Columbia River

Rocky Mountains

Missouri River

British Territory

Spanish Territory

Louisiana Territory

St. Charles, Missouri

Mississippi River

Ohio River

N
W E
S

Within a few days, they pass La Charrette. This is the last trading **outpost** they will see on their journey through the **frontier**.

This promises to be an amazing adventure!

THE HEARTLAND OF AMERICA

Heave!

Traveling against the swift currents of the Missouri River is tiring work. The men often have to tow the boats from the shore.

Sandbars are a constant danger. They slow the expedition's progress and risk damaging valuable supplies.

Unload the supplies before they're destroyed!

The men also face other dangers. Ticks and similar insects trouble the group. Many men develop skin rashes and sicknesses.

Ugh. I feel awful!

Progress is slow, but the land is beautiful. Walnut, ash, and cottonwood trees grow along the river. The countryside is full of wildlife.

Both Lewis and Clark keep journals of the expedition. Clark fills his with drawings of the animals they encounter.

Clark also creates maps. He draws small maps in his journal and larger ones on big sheets of paper.

Lewis collects samples of the new plants and animals the group sees. He plans to send these back to President Jefferson.

Those flowers are real beauties, Seaman!

The president will be excited to see this!

September 17, 1804:
The group reaches the **Great Plains** of present-day Nebraska and South Dakota. Large herds of buffalo, deer, elk, and pronghorn roam the land.

In late September, the explorers meet with the Teton Sioux.

But the party does not share a language with the **Native** Americans. They give gifts and use hand signals to communicate.

The Tetons do not want the explorers to trade directly with tribes upstream. They are unwilling to let the group pass.

They're trying to steal the boat! Stop them!

After four long days, the **stalemate** finally ends. Lewis and Clark give the Tetons more gifts. The expedition pushes westward.

October 8, 1804:
The group meets with the Arikara tribe in South Dakota and exchanges gifts.

In late October, the party arrives in Mandan and Hidatsa homelands in central North Dakota.

Our government wants to be friends with your people. We've brought medals as signs of peace.

November 3, 1804:
With winter quickly approaching, Lewis and Clark decide to stay near the Mandan and Hidatsa tribes. They build a series of cabins and sheds. They name it **Fort** Mandan.

For food, the men hunt buffalo. They often go out in below-zero temperatures.

Careful! Watch your step on the ice!

During the winter, Lewis and Clark hire Toussaint Charbonneau, a French-Canadian trader, and his wife, Sacagawea, as **interpreters**. They will join the explorers on the journey west.

11

INTO THE UNKNOWN

April 7, 1805:
The group leaves Fort Mandan. The keelboat, loaded with samples and journals, heads back to St. Louis. From there, its cargo will be shipped to President Jefferson.

The Corps of Discovery continues toward present-day Montana. The group now consists of 33 people, six canoes, and two pirogues.

April 25, 1805:
Lewis travels ahead of the main group to the Yellowstone River to **survey** the land.

April 29, 1805:
Lewis has a dangerous encounter with two grizzly bears. One of the bears chases him.

The land seems to stretch forever, Seaman.

It must weigh almost 300 pounds!

That was a close one!

June 13, 1805:
The group reaches the Great Falls of the Missouri River. The expedition must **portage** its supplies and boats around the falls by land.

It is the grandest sight I have ever beheld.

The explorers build wagons to carry their canoes. They find the rocky ground is full of cacti. Their shoes offer little protection.

The portage takes nearly a month to complete. Then Lewis and Clark have an important decision to make.

We need to find a guide to get us through the Rockies.

Yeah, we'll be doomed if we get trapped here during the winter.

The captains decide to search for the Shoshone tribe, whom they have heard will help them. Lewis presses on ahead, while Clark stays back. He has fallen ill and will catch up to Lewis later.

August 13, 1805:
Lewis's party locates the Shoshone village. They are warmly greeted by the Shoshone chief, Cameahwait.

Several days later, Clark's party reaches the village. Sacagawea embraces the chief. He is her brother.

What a stroke of good luck!

August 20, 1805:

There is no easy water route to the Columbia River.

But there is a trail through the Rockies used by the Nez Perce tribe.

The captains cross the mountains on horses bought from the Shoshone tribe. Old Toby, a Shoshone guide, leads the way.

By September 10, the group reaches the rugged Bitterroot Mountains, part of the Rockies. Wet, cold, and low on food, the party struggles onward.

September 20, 1805:
Clark and several hunters leave the main group and find a Nez Perce village. There they trade for fish and other foods. Two days later, the entire group meets at the village. They have finally crossed the Rockies.

Over the next two weeks, the group makes new canoes and trades for food from the Native Americans. On October 7, the group is on the move again.

We will care for your horses during the winter. You can pick them up on your return trip.

On October 16, the group finally reaches the Columbia River. One week later, they enter a 55-mile stretch of river with dangerous rapids and falls.

November 7, 1805:

Ocean in view! O! the joy!

However, the group is still several miles from the ocean. They have only arrived at the **estuary** of the Columbia River.

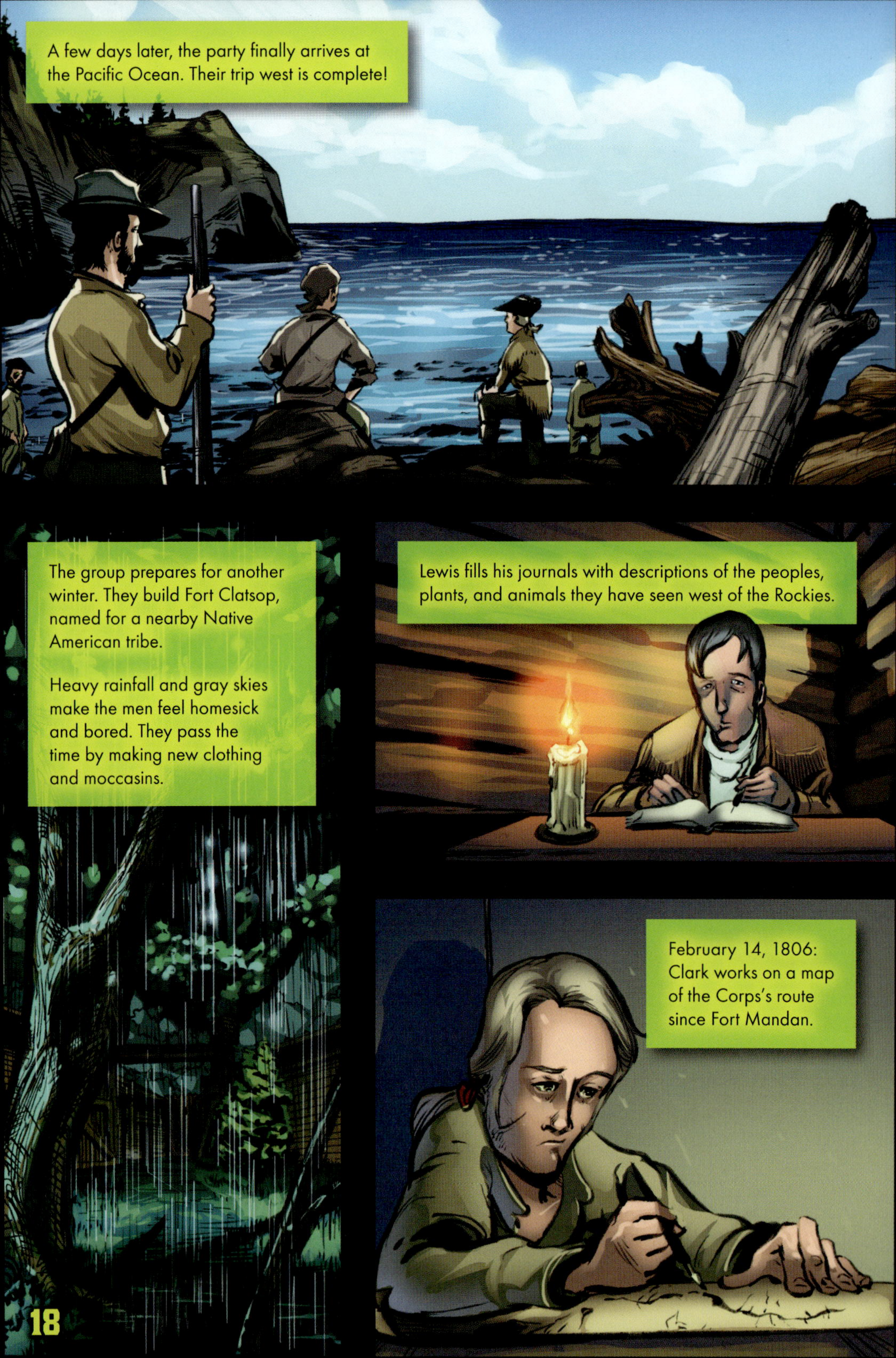

A few days later, the party finally arrives at the Pacific Ocean. Their trip west is complete!

The group prepares for another winter. They build Fort Clatsop, named for a nearby Native American tribe.

Heavy rainfall and gray skies make the men feel homesick and bored. They pass the time by making new clothing and moccasins.

Lewis fills his journals with descriptions of the peoples, plants, and animals they have seen west of the Rockies.

February 14, 1806: Clark works on a map of the Corps's route since Fort Mandan.

Going Home

The party follows the Columbia River east. The journey is filled with portages and little food.

On July 3, 1806, the captains split up the party. Lewis's group searches for a shortcut back to the Missouri River. Clark leads a group to the Yellowstone River.

On July 25, Clark arrives at Pompey's Pillar in present-day Montana. He carves his name and date on the rock.

Lewis's group has a violent run-in with the Blackfoot tribe. The explorers hurry toward the Missouri River to rejoin Clark's group.

August 12, 1806: When the two parties meet, Lewis is hurt. He has been shot by a crewmember in a hunting accident.

Luckily, you have no broken bones.

I'll manage. It could have been worse!

August 14, 1806: The party reaches the Mandan and Hidatsa villages where they spent the first winter.

It's good to be home!

September 17, 1806:
The voyage home continues quickly, but the captains receive surprising news when they meet a U.S. Army captain.

We had all given up on you. We thought you were dead!

I'm sure President Jefferson has hopes for us yet!

It's La Charrette!

We're almost home!

September 23, 1806, noon:
The party arrives at St. Louis, Missouri. In two years, four months, and ten days, the Corps of Discovery has traveled nearly 8,000 miles. They became friends with many of the Native American tribes they met. They also learned much about the land and wildlife in the new territory.

More About the Lewis and Clark Expedition

- France sold the Louisiana Territory to the United States for $15 million. France needed the money to go to war with Great Britain.

- The territory included 828,000 square miles (2,144,510 square kilometers). This land more than doubled the size of the United States. It later became all or part of 15 states.

- Sergeant Charles Floyd was the only man on the expedition to die during the trip. Floyd suffered appendicitis and passed away on August 20, 1804.

- To prepare for the expedition, Lewis studied the sciences at universities in Philadelphia, Pennsylvania.

- The group discovered about 120 previously undocumented animals. These included the white-tailed deer, sea otter, mountain goat, grizzly bear, and red fox. They also found nearly 200 new types of plants.

Glossary

corps—an organized group of people

estuary—an area where a river meets an ocean

expedition—a trip made for a specific purpose

fort—a settlement where soldiers or explorers live

frontier—an area where few people live

Great Plains—a large area of prairie between the Missouri River and Rocky Mountains

interpreters—people who can speak for others who do not know the same language

keelboat—a shallow riverboat that is usually rowed or towed

native—originally from a specific place

outpost—a small town far from other cities

pirogues—small boats similar to canoes

portage—carrying boats and supplies on land from one body of water to another

sandbars—raised areas of sand near the surface of a body of water

stalemate—a situation where no progress or advantage is possible

survey—to measure or examine the land

To Learn More

AT THE LIBRARY

Domnauer, Teresa. *The Lewis & Clark Expedition*. New York, N.Y.: Children's Press, 2013.

Raum, Elizabeth. *Expanding a Nation: Causes and Effects of the Louisiana Purchase*. North Mankato, Minn.: Capstone Press, 2014.

Stille, Darlene R. *The Journals of Lewis and Clark*. Chicago, Ill.: Heinemann Library, 2013.

ON THE WEB

Learning more about Lewis and Clark is as easy as 1, 2, 3.

1. Go to www.factsurfer.com.
2. Enter "Lewis and Clark" into the search box.
3. Click the "Surf" button and you will see a list of related web sites.

With factsurfer.com, finding more information is just a click away.

Index